THE NAMES
OF A HARE
IN ENGLISH

DAVID YOUNG

Published by the University of Pittsburgh Press, Pittsburgh, Pa., 15260
Copyright © 1979, David Young
Feffer and Simons, Inc., London
Manufactured in the United States of America

Library of Congress Cataloging in Publication Data

Young, David P.
   The names of a hare in English.

  (Pitt poetry series)
  I. Title.
PS3575.O78N3   811'.5'4   79-4704
ISBN 0-8229-3406-X
ISBN 0-8229-5311-0 pbk.

Acknowledgment is made to the following publications for permission to re-
print poems that appear in this book: *Grove, Kayak, The Missouri Review,
New Honolulu Review, Pocket Pal,* and *Poetry Now.* "The Picture Says," pp.
20-21, © 1979 The New Yorker Magazine, Inc. "After My Death," "The
Names of a Hare in English," and "Two Views of the Cathedral" first
appeared in *Poetry.*

The publication of this book is supported by a grant from the National Endowment for the Arts in Washington, D.C., a Federal agency.

For Newell
and Margaret

CONTENTS

THE NAMES
OF A HARE
IN ENGLISH

TWO VIEWS OF THE CATHEDRAL

1. Day

Shoulderstones, blockstacks, peaks:
we put it up to catch our breath.
Thumbs, antlers, ferns and flying bones:
we put it up to catch the light.
A million thorns to house a rose,
another mask for god. And then a mind
hushed for the few thin sounds of dream:
the knicker-knack of pigeons in the frieze,
the lunk of something closing in the crypt,
while a woman folds a large white cloth
in the wet yard behind the apse.

2. *Night*

Uneven candle crescent round the Virgin.
Casket time. The verger sees his breath.
High in the nave, the hunchback sees it all:
history is a slow march down the aisle, is
the countess sobbing in her heavy cloak.
Here a knight sat and felt his throat
fill up with blood. A crunch under my boot;
frost? mortar? salt? I tip my forehead back:
no roof, just dusty stars above . . .
We build. On the numb stone called fear
we fit the heavy one called love.

3

Dragging a rake, my Uncle Donald
surveys his Victory Garden:

peaceful and green,
all Minneapolis is at war . . .

since I am seven, that's mostly
cereal box Messerschmitts,
Tojo cartoons, the bombers I draw
sailing through popcorn flak,
bad dreams, brownouts,

and the small cigarette machine
my father and Donald roll smokes with
as they sit up to grumble
at Roosevelt, winning again . . .

Countries of silence. Hand on my heart
I moon to return, searching for signs,
gnats in November, submarines
at rest on the harbor floor.

Then all at once I have done it!
I stand on the corner of Queen Street.
Five o'clock. The nations of the dead.
Mr. Kipke is whistling for his cat
and a light shines across the street
in the bedroom of the boy
with the bullet-shattered spine.

I sidle, thrilled, down our alley,
floating, loose as a ghost.
At our picket gate I find
my father, his back to me.

Is he pondering the war
or my brother, soon to be born?
I could touch his shoulder and ask him
but both of us are fading
as the city shines, all mystery,
and the garden sits empty in twilight:
pine needles, vines, brown leaves,
simple American shadows.

"OTHER FORMS WERE NEAR":
FIVE WORDS

HONEYGUT (a word for tripe)

Below the graded greens of tree, bush, weeds,
it's silent—barn-cathedrals of quiet, but
no space: rooms all wall, jampacked with roots (white sprays,
hard tentacles), pebbles, sandgrains, humus,
tigerstriped tons of rock, pods of water and gas . . .

When you wake in the morning, rumpled and stunned,
the crumbs around your eyes are there to tell you
where you were lying all night, what you were practicing.

OAT

Yeats stands near his old-hat tower in the twilight;
everything talks to itself—the river over its rocks, the moorhens,
cricket and cowbell, wind in the chimney flue. What he's gaping at:
the Great Pyramid, trembling like a bubble above the trees.

"Willie is booming and buzzing like a bumblebee,"
said Maud Gonne to a friend. "That means he is writing something."
Who can he talk to when he's neither here nor there? Mumbling,
gaping. As the specters billow and fade. Ripe mummy wheat.

BABOON

Today a summer thundershower makes her think
of packs of sacred apes. Long hair, a kind of skidding run.
Isn't the animal mirror best? Those hours in the zoo
watching the young gorilla's hands: black leather work gloves.

The trees drip very strangely.
A robin runs across the lawn.

Bright eye.   Serpent mound.
The breathing next to your ear.

HAZE

Old, you were dozing at a window and woke up.
A stranger stood in the yard, the moon behind him,
so that you couldn't see his face. Then you recalled

watching a kingfisher from a canalboat: it was as if
that blue pulse tore straight through you. We're best

when the world shines us through like that. At night,
knee-deep in mist, the traveler pauses at a cottage,
straining to catch his face in the empty casement.

INSECT

Cow skull, washtub. Sunday-supplement portrait. Gloomy
    greatness.
The poem's place in the world was "never in dispute,"
they said. Any more than a blizzard. Or a candle.

When the dead walk, do they need to use their feet?
How gradual it seems, going to sleep each night,
instar after instar. I pace my study, looking for a book.
The snowstorm settles in its globe. The small bright flame
is nearly independent of its wick.

10

HOW MUSIC BEGAN

Well the wind blew so hard
that the sea blistered and snapped.
Even the boulders were squeaking.

Trolls scuffled and spat, whacking thick
bones on hollow oaks, screaming for meat,
and birds nattered in every thicket.

Women in birth pangs howled. Bitter couples
shattered cups, jugs and beakers, while children
slithered on ice among grit and cinders.

✿

Then thunder set off the landslide.
Bushes with dead birds tumbled
through blasted air. You couldn't hear

how bones and trees were splintered,
how boulders struck sparks, how the ice
burst, taking some of the children.

✿

Then quiet grew up. Like cave pools,
cocoons. Like very old temples at noon.
Nursing. Fruitfall. Sketching the buffalo.

And then it was easy to consider
smoke a bird twisting up
that might sing as the earth got smaller.

THREE TIME-TRIPS

1

My shoes crush acorns.
I'm thirty-nine I'm seven.
Far down the yard
my father and a neighbor
sail horseshoes through the air.

The clank and settle.

And the past I thought would dwindle
arcs back to me, a hoop.

The men wipe their necks,
the boy walks round the oak:
sometimes our lives rust gently,
a long-handled shovel, leaned
against a sun-warmed wall.

2

Fourteen, I perch on the wicker seat
in a nimbus of misery, love's shrimp,
hearing the streetcar's crackle and hiss
as the drugstore turns on its corner.

And what was real? The whipped sparks,
the glove puppets, bobbing, the pocket dreams,
this poem-to-be, my father's wharf
of set belief, the wicker and shellac?

Learning to be imperfect —
that's erudition!
Like coolies in flooded fields,
we wade on our own reflections.

3

November bleach and brownout. Acid sky,
falsetto sunlight, wire and fluff of weeds, pods,
bone and paper grass-clumps. The dog bounds off,
stitching the field with her nose. Hound city.

It's thirteen years. Different dog, same field,
and double grief: dull for the slumped president,
stake-sharp for my friend's ripped heart—faint
night-cries in the mansions where we lived.

But the bullet grooves are gone, the first dog's dead,
and here is the field, seedy and full of sameness.
Speech fails, years wrinkle. Dream covers dream

that covered dream. My head starts up a jazz
I never could concoct. I have to grin. On the cold pond
the tinsmith wind is whistling at his work.

ONE WHO CAME BACK

I can't be sure
why we should want you among us

you with your bruised clothes
your fingers thickened by pity

terror's night watchman, mopping blood
where the books lie stitched with quiet

who stood in the grass near the graves
striking the match of darkness

but I know we seem to need you
the way we do bread or warmth

so I'm out here in the moonlight
pounding nails in your footprints

as if that could make you stay.

1

I looked up from my weeding
and saw a butterfly, coal black,
floating across Plum Creek. Which facts
are laced with lies: it was another day,
it was a monarch—if it was black,
it must have been incinerator fluff.

A black hinge, opening and shutting.

2

Elsewhere the sunset lights
bonfires in hotel windows, gilds the lake,
picks out false embers where it can:
watch crystal, drinking glass, earring.
"Nabokov," someone calls, "is dead . . ."
What would you give to be in, say, Fialta,
hearing the rhythms of a torpid coast?
Or on the porch at the Enchanted Hunters,
conversing in the shadows with Sirin?
Sneezes, lachrymose sighs. Chuckles and coughs.
When at a loss for words, try waving
one helpless hand before your face.

Walking the dog, I saw a hawkmoth too,
big as two hands, resting under a streetlight.

3

In the skyscraper across the lane
an aproned man sets up his easel
at the window opposite, and cocks his head.
What does he see? A dwarf
mixing a violet powder, a fat
landlady playing Patience, a little girl
brushing a velvet coat, in tears,
three people having sex. In short,
the world. Ourselves. Aren't all of us
some form of Maxwell's Demon,
particle sorters, systems
so self-enclosed they work too well to work?
Grandmaster, slip into your fiction like
Houdini diving through a pocket mirror.
Here's wonder, but no grief. And even so,
you'd not have liked this poem. Wan child
in a sailor suit, man running by
waving a gauzy net, tall fencer, pedant,
hotelmensch, empty suit of clothes . . .

One exile more. One language still to learn.

OCCUPATIONAL HAZARDS

Butcher
If I want to go to pieces
I can do that. When I try
to pull myself together
I get sausage.

Bakers
Can't be choosers. Rising
from a white bed, from dreams
of kings, bright cities, buttocks,
to see the moon by daylight.

Tailor
It's not the way the needle
drags the poor thread around.
It's sewing the monster together,
my misshapen son.

Gravediggers
To be the baker's dark opposite,
to dig the anti-cake, to stow
the sinking loaves in the unoven —
then to be dancing on the job!

Woodcutter
Deep in my hands
as far as I can go
the fallen trees
keep ringing.

THE PICTURE SAYS

1

That we all die, sometimes
when we are children.

That it would look like sleep
if flesh did not decay.

That we are marble, mottled,
that we are piebald clouds.

That we lie in the long grass,
peaceful, hair a little tangled,

grass like wires, spindles, rims,
grass like crisscross lifelines,

paths of the shooting stars,
arcs on the flecked night sky.

2

Sound of a backhoe, tractor-chug:
this old man is the pond digger—

he stands by the water's edge
on his open palm a pond-snail . . .

he is humming, a kind of bee-speech,
while the child sleeps in the grass

the water a grainy mirror,
the light, the smoky lilies,

and the sky, filling slowly
with bruise-blue rainclouds.

JAYWALKER

His arm leaves a dent in my hood.

He lies on the pavement, smiling
to reassure me.
                    Weeks later
the leak in his brain begins.
I try to imagine his headaches,
the murmuring nurses, the priest.
By then he is dead.

❋

Twenty-two years. I can't
remember his face or name.
He came from a farm across the river.
We tried to visit his father and mother.

Tonight it's as though
my brakes have failed
and I roll through the hushed sirens
past white faces, past
the weary Night Dispatcher, steering
my old, slow Mercury toward
the figure across the river,
the boy from the empty farmhouse
with his smile, his trick headaches.

I would like to light him a candle.
I would like to bring him a drink of water.
I would like to yield the right of way.
I would like to call across the river.

"It's all right now?" I'd shout.

His head would bob in the wind.

WISHING THE GIFT OF NARRATIVE

1

The story I told my children
had a magic pigeon, a gruff boatman,
and a cave beneath the sea
with a friend who gave off light
and a monster called the Ice-Mother
from whom they escaped with . . .
with what? That story was so happy
we all began to forget it.

Then that's no story, that's a memory.

2

At the birth of the Virgin
all was confusion—too many
women crowding the chamber
and too much water: basins and wine jars
flourished in every corner
and none was allowed to escape
by leaping from heat in the quick
rhythms of steam. They say
it was all spring snow
and very recently melted.

That's no story, that's a picture.

3

It seems that murderous samurai
nailed his wife to a door
and threw it into the river,
and when her apparition
came to him in the mountains
he naturally went berserk
and was eaten by a lion
who had been sleeping in the peonies.
"Another trick on death," he said
as his head poked out from the lion's jaws.

That's no story, that's a joke.

4

What do you see in your mirror
that makes your hair rise slowly
until it's a black wheatfield?
And how could you be indifferent
to the waterfall? Jack Bat
the neighborhood sybarite
pillowed his head on your navel
and gazed, as you slept, at the moon
which seemed to speak firmly, saying:
"Go down to the stone bridge.
I'll pick you up next winter."

That's no story, that's just a mystery.

5

The snowy owl swooped from the woods
to perch on the hen-house roof
and the angel who cares about barnyards
folded his long arms and sighed . . .

Yes, I admit, that's good
but I want to be told a story
that is music drifting over river lights
men being happy and harmless
and great clouds sailing overhead
gliding toward you like ancestors
with arms outstretched, faces polished . . .

All good stories, then, are they about death?

Yes, death. And life. Yes. Life and Death.

*Death and Life were husband and wife
and they lived in a hut on the moon.*

Time puts an arm around me. I feel proud!
Another story's begun!

for Diane Vreuls

25

DECEMBER FOURTH, 1974

Rainer Maria Rilke,
on this your ninety-ninth birthday
I make you the following presents:

a woodpecker's egg
roasted
in the flame of a small candle

an art nouveau jug
half full
from the wounds of your pretty
saints

the finger of a mummy
that will always point the way

a cloud of organ
sound a cloud
of orange and gold
butterflies
circling a pillar of salt

the nose of a pony that's
a trumpet a muscle a loaf

a poem by Tu Fu
that goes off like an old musket

the stunned
chain pickerel
I caught in a net this fall

oh the great big poppy of metaphor

the past and future for which you exchanged
my present your
present

I give it back, your present
that I keep losing and finding
red thread
angel's knuckle
smoke in the rafters   crows

STRAW AND WHAT FOLLOWS

Crate shapes stacked on a truck
as if dry shine and slippery tickle
could be squared off I put my hand inside
and touched a leathermouse a bat can smell
hot tractors and wet pens shot hogs a horse
noses my coat in a book I read a woman felt
a man's weight pressing down and from beneath
prickle of hay on her thighs puzzling about
delight I ride the piled bales behind my uncle
weaving a cornhusk crown stitching a nest
while wind as unconcerned as monks or moss
snitches my bleached and hardly raveled hat
and rolls across three fields of switching cows

TOOL TALK

Put tip of pot through loop. Pull tight.
Call this position B. File flash and sand.
Use adze to strike off wobbly-pump
of Handley-Page or Spad. Dry roller stocks,
make notch in carrick bits with extra pick
and fit in spindle bush. Dash for the churn,
dash for the peak. Lakes equal paddles, bridles
are for camels, skies, a harness punch will fix
my son's new watch or fill that ladle in the stable.
Fit pitching chisel into granite crotch: release.
If cannon diagram does not apply, destroy.
Let sun god slide through threading lathe. Tie
lightning rod with thong. Work corks in slots of loom.
Rewind. Let sonnet slide from side to side.

AFTER MY DEATH

1

It will all go backward. Leaves
that fell in October will float up
and gather in trees for greening.
The fire I built will pull
its smoke back in while the logs
blaze and grow whole. Lost hailstones
will freeze themselves back into beads,
bounce once and rise up in a storm,
and as flowers unwilt and then tighten to buds
and the sun goes back toward where it rose
I will step out through shrinking grass
at one for the first time
with my own breath, the wax
and wane of moon, dewsoak, tidewheel,
the kiss of puddle and star.

2

It will all go on. Rimefrost, mist;
at the cracked mirror the janitor
will comb his hair and hum, three boys
will build a raft, chalk dust will settle
in blackboard troughs, trucks bump
on the railroad crossing, soft talk in trees,
a girl practicing her fiddle: I know this,
I keep imagining it, or trying, and sometimes
when I try hard, it is a small stone fern
delicate, changeless, heavy in my hand.
And then it weighs nothing
and then it is green
and everything is breathing.

A LOWERCASE ALPHABET

a   snail going up the wall

b   hang up the little dipper

c   mouth, moon, riverbend

d   the dipper in the mirror

e   tiny eye of the whale

f   oil well, skate, old pistol

g   what did you do to your glasses?

h   a chimney for every hut

i   the levitation of the spot

j   landscape with fishhook and planet

k   where three roads almost meet

l   romance of the periscope

m   comb from the iron age

n	the hut that lost its chimney
o	simplification of the blood
p	the dipper dead and buried
q	its mirror buried with it
r	geyser that goes off crooked
s	little black love seat
t	the portable cross
u	cross section of a trough
v	the hawk above the valley
w	a graph for winter, pigsfoot
x	dancer, hourglass, black suspenders
y	the root begins to sprout
z	path of the rabbit

THE FOOL'S TALE

When I said good-night to the old gaffer
he suddenly flew away laughing!

In the woods I came on a blood-red boar
and a burnt hunter, locked in a stare,

as at Christmas when animals fell on their knees
while the nail and the hammer told them lies.

Magic! So much! You clutch your poor head,
a barrel of rainberries falls from a cloud,

a dwarf whose face is covered with fur
steals your watch, purse, and painted guitar

and a very great darkness covers the earth,
thunder and lightning live at your hearth . . .

No! Hush! It's gone absolutely still—
the stone drops forever into the well,

and a sly little girl with a hood and a muff
walks down the road with a timber wolf.

The Names of a Hare in English

Les nouns de un levre en Engleis

The mon that the hare i-met
Ne shal him nevere be the bet,
Bot if he lei down on londe
That he bereth in his honde,
(Be hit staf, he hit bouwe),
And blesce him with his helbowe.
And mid wel goed devosioun
He shall saien on oreisoun
In the worshipe of the hare
Thenne mai he wel fare.

"The hare, the scotart,
The bigge, the bouchart,
The scotewine, the skikart,
The turpin, the tirart,
The wei-betere, the ballart,
The go-bi-dich, the soillart,
The wimount, the babbart,
The stele-awai, the momelart,
The evil-i-met, the babbart,
The scot, the deubert,
The gras-bitere, the goibert,
The late-at-hom, the swikebert,
The frendlese, the wodecat,
The brodlokere, the bromkat,
The purblinde, the fursecat,
The louting, the westlokere,
The waldenlie, the sid-lokere,
And eke the roulekere;
The stobhert, the long-here,
The strau-der, the lekere
The wilde der, the lepere
The shorte der, the lorkere,

36

The wint-swift, the sculkere,
The hare serd, the heg-roukere,
The deudinge, the deu-hoppere,
The sittere, the gras-hoppere,
The fitelfot, the foldsittere,
The ligtt-fot, the fernsittere,
The cawel-hert, the wortcroppere,
The go-bi-ground, the sitte-stille,
The pintail, the toure-tohulle;
The cove-arise,
The make-agrise,
The wite-wombe,
The go-mit-lombe,
The choumbe, the chaulart,
The chiche, the couart,
The make-fare, the breke-forwart,
The fnattart, the pollart,
(His hei nome is srewart);
The hert with the letherene hornes,
The der that woneth in the cornes,
The der that alle men scornes,
The der that no-mon ne-dar nemmen."

When thou havest al this i-said,
Thenne is the hare migtt alaid.
Thenne migtt thou wenden forth,
Est and west, and south and north,
Wedrewardes so mon wile,
The man that con ani skile.
Have nou godne dai, sire hare!
God the lete so wel fare,
That thou come to me ded,
Other in cive, other in bred! Amen!

—MS Digby 86f 168 v. (1272–1283)

1

Just an old poem. Beyond us,
worn as a bone—but this one
seems to keep doubling back.
Look: fresh tracks, a crosspath. Nervous,
I glance around, I want to know
who wrote it. What liar would claim
seventy-some names for
the pop-eyed, great-hearted
cousin of the rabbit?

I think I know what happened.
I get these fits myself.
For a moment language is everything,
a path to the heart, a small
city of stars on the tongue:
then everything looks in the mirror
and sees his cool twin nothing . . .
seventy names are none.

2

In the time before dawn, in graylight,
a fur purse hops through the soaked grass,
a stump stands by a stump and then is gone;
this is the time when names are none and many,
the time when names themselves have names.

Say the word, things happen.
Say the long hare is a deer, there's
a crash in the bracken. Say
fiddlefoot, you hear pounding
on the packed door of the earth.

Prospero stands in his sour ring,
somebody else's fict. "Turpin,"
he whispers, and a small
furzecat appears at his feet.
"Dewbert," he says, and now
there are two, sidelookers,
late-at-homes, the master smiles,
says "Budget," there are four,
says "Hedgecroucher" and
there are eight but
you know how this
story comes out . . .

What do we have for animal magic
but names, our mumbled spells and charms,
baskets of epithets spilled down the page?

A straw deer stood here
right at this line
but a grassbiter ate it
and then a broomcat swept it away

a windswift blew or flew to where
the westlooker stood looking east
toward the wastelooker in his hair
shirt, but
you know how this goes
you turn the corner of the line
and startle a fernsitter who evaporates
now you see him now
you don't now you name him now . . .

3

Along the Vermilion River
the farmer's wife points out some shallow caves
where slaves hid on the way to Canada
and Indians rested, migrating south.
Settlers stood on the bank and watched,
I figure, as I do, hands in my pockets,
wanting to belong to this, or it to me.

An old woman with us knows
the name of every plant.
"What's this?" I ask, testing her.
"Mary's Bedstraw," she says!
I'm shivering. To know the name,
to possess and be possessed!
Don't apologize. Wild Geranium, Dog Violet,
Sneezewort, Bloodroot, Jack-in-the-Pulpit,
so we trail through the river-bottom woods
and names bind us to strange forms of life.
A good new name, I tell myself,
is what the farmer feels, turning
an arrowhead or axehead up.
His hand closes around the past,
the mystery of why he's here;
the world extends too far
and yet he's in it, holding a small rock!

We pace on through the woods. Trillium everywhere,
stars on a green spring evening,
bones in an Irish pasture.

4

And what's the rain's name?
Certainly not cloudcurd, aireggs.

A bear staggers through the raspberry canes,
a crow feather falls through a noontime pine,
a pail of yellow oil tips into a cistern.
Rain walks down the gangplank, waving.
Climbs windbreaks. Stipples windows. Freckles sand.
The farmhands' faces glisten, yes

that name is right. The one name. Rain.

5

We have some quiet families in this neighborhood.
Constellations, let's start from there. Bear, Plough,
Charles's Wain, how choose? Pleiades: better
as Seven Sisters, but I like Hen and Chickens best.
Is that Pandora, lid-lifting? No, President Taft,
strolling with his cigar. Andromeda,
chained lady? How about Rita Hayworth's
Iceboat? Go on, make up your own,
holding a child's hand, saying: See, there's Moth.
Glove. Submarine. Malcolm's X.
Chandelier. Cottontail. Moebius' Strip: God's Ring.

Well, drop your head.
The field's still here, with its milk vetch and thistles,
the house with its one lamp lit.

6

eye,

strange that your name should be an ideogram,
two peepers with a crooked beak between;
and on beyond the thing itself
a jelly bleb, bubble of stare,
loll-in-a-socket, goggle-in-a-purse,
the little leak that floods the cave:

I came to the rim of the crater
to see where it lay asleep
under its flaps and dark spike fence,
work never stops in the observatory,
then it jumped open and I ran home,
back to the name, hearing behind me:

> I am blue. My name is Helen.
> Haply I squeeze a tear
> and it rolls away with a wet spoor.
> In the dark hole where all of you go
> you will not need me. See?

7

Shakespeare's portrait hangs in my office.
The round, poised face, balding and bone-yellow,
hovers on its ruff against
a dark brown background. Lately
when I glance up it is
my father's face. And I am pleased. Afraid.
What the prince told the ghost flares a second
against brown sky: *I'll call thee . . . father.*

My father's alive and well
in Minneapolis. His business
was business, but the other day
he gazed at me from a dust jacket
in Wallace Stevens' look. That's dangerous,
that father-saying. A breath huffs, jaw drops,
tongue jumps between teeth. To say
I'll call, I'll call you, I'll call *you*
father. And call. And you. Then
they start to call you father. What a name.
A cloak, a jacket.
You take it off.
Your head floats off the ruff. Your gaze
travels. Your sons wince.

8

I look at the backs of my hands and get lost:
an old wind bends the grass, blue trails fan
from wrist to flushed and cross-hatched knuckles;
stand on one, look out along
the five peninsulas, ridges crossed
by ravelins and runnels, at the tips
the slick nails flaring; you could do
a tap dance, smiling, and fall off . . .

I look at my hands, searching for their names,
picker and stealer, Guildenstern and Rosencrantz,
the scarred serf who dropped the crystal goblets,
the oldest cups, the simplest maps,
furrow-makers, strangling partners, fist and claw,
smoothing the child's hair, poking shadows,
wringing laundry, helpless in sleep. I look
at my hands. How could they have names?

9

The dogs were barking over at the pigfarm,
the leaftruck was crawling through autumn,
lovers were unbuttoning in cellars
and what was I up to in that badlit attic?

I sat sewing my own name to my arm.
Young? What thing is Young? I was going
to help the spelling of wrinkles, welts,
scar tissue, crowsfeet, veinscript, I'd be
my hospital wristband, walking dogtag, and when
my palms and their spidery letters were gone,
scrotum and brain with their intricate scribbles,
I hoped my bone-bald cranium, somebody's paperweight,
would show its old faint Y. If I couldn't
be the Book, I could at least
be one or two of the letters.

10

One time,
he came through the trees in a helmet.
We couldn't see his eyes. There were long-needled pines:
at each needle's tip stood a round drop
catching the light. When we looked back
whoever was there had vanished.

And from the hill
we watched him mowing the meadow.
His sleeves were rolled up. A horse
stood patient, hitched to a gig.
It was like watching the river
racing among its rocks.

Was it
near the empty factory you heard him?
A fear-stab: faintly
he was singing inside. Brick dust
sifted, cinders crunched under boots.
You didn't know the song, you didn't
know his name. Oil in a puddle,
when you were a child, made rainbows. Your face
wore the same soft fascinated look
when the bonfire made sparks that spiraled up
and then were gone.

11

It got away again:

"the deer with the leathery horns
the deer that lives in the corns
the deer that all men scorns
the deer that no one dares to name"

Names, get between me and the things I fear.
Names, for godsake tell me who I am.

Nothing and everything. The time comes
when you shut the door, step off the porch
and walk across the fields without a word.

12

A day swings past. A husk of hares
disappears over the hill. Dawn again.
I've looked at the small change in my pocket:
eye, star, hand, rain,
father, mirror, bedstraw, bloodroot.
Now, doing my act I find a bone,
step in the sour circle, find
the bone knows how to sing:

> "Fowles in the frith
>   The fisses in the flod,
> And I mon waxe wod.
>   Mulch sorwe I walk with
> For best of bon and blood."

Fishes in the flood, and I could go mad:
language, that burrow, warren, camouflage,
language will deceive you and survive you.

Well then, so what?
I look up *frith*.

Oh game preserve of words!
Oh goldfinch feeding in the buttonbush!
The dogs of death are loosed
upon that little rabbit, Metaphor,
but he can double back. And does.

Milne Holton and Paul Vangelisti, eds., *The New Polish Poetry: A Bilingual Collection*

David Huddle, *Paper Boy*

Shirley Kaufman, *The Floor Keeps Turning*

Shirley Kaufman, *From One Life to Another*

Shirley Kaufman, *Gold Country*

Abba Kovner, *A Canopy in the Desert: Selected Poems*

Paul-Marie Lapointe, *The Terror of the Snows: Selected Poems*

Larry Levis, *Wrecking Crew*

Jim Lindsey, *In Lieu of Mecca*

Tom Lowenstein, tr., *Eskimo Poems from Canada and Greenland*

Archibald MacLeish, *The Great American Fourth of July Parade*

Peter Meinke, *The Night Train and The Golden Bird*

James Moore, *The New Body*

Carol Muske, *Camouflage*

Gregory Pape, *Border Crossings*

Thomas Rabbitt, *Exile*

Belle Randall, *101 Different Ways of Playing Solitaire and Other Poems*

Ed Roberson, *Etai-Eken*

Ed Roberson, *When Thy King Is A Boy*

Eugene Ruggles, *The Lifeguard in the Snow*

Dennis Scott, *Uncle Time*

Herbert Scott, *Groceries*

Richard Shelton, *The Bus to Veracruz*

Richard Shelton, *Of All the Dirty Words*

Richard Shelton, *The Tattooed Desert*

Richard Shelton, *You Can't Have Everything*

Gary Soto, *The Elements of San Joaquin*

Gary Soto, *The Tale of Sunlight*

David Steingass, *American Handbook*

David Steingass, *Body Compass*

Tomas Tranströmer, *Windows & Stones: Selected Poems*

Alberta T. Turner, *Learning to Count*

Alberta T. Turner, *Lid and Spoon*

Marc Weber, *48 Small Poems*

Bruce Weigl, *A Romance*

David P. Young, *The Names of a Hare in English*

David P. Young, *Sweating Out the Winter*